D0209546

abecedarium

abecedarium

Peter Lamborn Wilson

2010

Xexoxial Editions

West Lima, Wisconsin

Cover art by Liaizon Wakest. All illustrations by Peter Lamborn Wilson.
Designed by mIEKAL aND December 2009
© Peter Lamborn Wilson 2010

ISBN 0-9770049-8-8
EAN-13 978-0-9770049-8-0

published by

Xexoxial Editions
10375 County Highway Alphabet
La Farge, WI 54639

perspicacity@xexoxial.org
www.xexoxial.org

for Zon

ABECEDARIUM

A commentary on *Mysteries of the Alphabet* by Rabbi M.-A. Ouaknin.

A

aleph

hieroglyph

proto - Sinaitic

Transition

A

Enraged bull lowers its head to charge. Making the sign against
the Evil Eye:

So the witch would see the letter A

(but doesn't see it because the
gesture remains concealed)

.

A floating story told about various sufis: -- as a child on the first
day of school he refuses to learn the alphabet beyond aleph --foolish
schoolmaster punishes him -- etc.

All bulls are the Apis Bull. But his horns remain erect: viz., the
neolithic altars, Çatal Hüyük, pre-Homeric Crete. He lowers his horns
only to charge the matador's cape. Blade slips into spine. But now the
Ox comes forth domesticated -- lowers its head to pull & strain at
waterwheel or plow. The first sound A-U-M, origin of the garland
of skulls.

B

beth

hieroglyph

Proto-Sineitic

transition

B

is for barn or byre or building or house -- perhaps cattle share
it with humans like in old Ireland. Maybe the ox isn't so much
coming forth as *going in* -- down into Egypt. Sounds have been
enclosed in rigid sounds -- A is A, B is B. Beneath them the
archaeographologue uncovers walls of old houses broken pottery
bones. What did they bury with the dead & why? Surely the dead have
provided these ruins with an immense gravity or suffocating
heaviness -- almost suction. These mummies are dehydrated & they
long for the blood of living words or even inarticulate sounds.

Without letters there could be no machines; what letters do for
sound the machine does for force. A machine is the sign of its own
operation. Nothing ever melts into something else.

Not that it isn't heimlich und gemütlich here inside. B is for
Beidermeier: without B there'd be no rainy November Viennese
coffeeshops with newspapers pinched between slats of split cane or
bamboo. Old Egyptian & Mesopotamian scribes sit in the shadows fading
in & out against the stained velvet settees. Sachertorte mit schlaag,
bitte. Civilization loses its predatory atmosphere, the coffee
smells so intelligent, like opium.

C

gimmel

hieroglyph

$\wedge\wedge$

proto-Sinaitic

$\wedge$ $\wedge$ (neck or hump?)

L LL

Transition

L < C

C

for camel. I have a hieroglyph of it right here on the table
in front of me. Sometime try standing on a busy corner in a daytime
city & count how many images of animals you can see. Good to think
with. Nineteenth century New York was far more polluted with
horseshit than anything else. Use the letters (each with its
built-in animal) & discard the mess of animate nature.

Invariably we come back to Gnostic imagery: sparks of light incased
& prisoned in shells of dead matter -- or rather in abstract forms.
You can scarcely call them "arbitrary" -- every single alphabet in
the world is rooted in this same handful of Egyptian pictograms.

The camel is always setting out on a journey. Even before
domestication it liked to travel. As autumn approaches you can hear
distant camel bells: caravans depart for the nomadic sphere: Jonathan
Chapman, cherubinic wanderer, fool of the Tarot. The Camel not the
Wheel. Ibn Khaldun says wool & hair & fur of wild animals possess
more aura than domesticates: -- bedouin dialectic. Jade, silk, tea,
the emergence of Capitalism on the margin between settled &
unsettled.

Nomadism: safety valve for civilization's discontents. Tourism tries to serve the same function but fails because it erodes difference instead of reinforcing it.

If you move much faster than a camel you don't really move, you destroy distance. Distance equals freedom, so freedom equals slowness. Freedom means to leave the house, but the alphabet makes it unnecessary, and without necessity there can exist (by contrast) no release from necessity, no freedom. Not the idea of the camel but the camel itself, spitting & honking its way across the desert.

Each of the letters kills the thing it has replaced.

D

daleth

hieroglyph

Sabaean   (tent door)

hieroglyph   (fish head)

(vulva = breast)

Transition   D

D

for Door or vulva the body's door. The way in is the way out. Cabalistic or hermeto-critical praxis precludes any pure negative approach to alphabetic symbolism -- even tho *this* ABC stresses spectral rather than formal aspects of alphabetism. No idyllic return to pre-literacy. There's nothing particularly "oral" about radio & TV since they could never have been invented without the machine of letters in the first place.

Why have most of these signs been turned around, down, upside down? According to Prof. Ouaknin the process of alphabetization consists of a Mosaic attempt to purify the pagan pictograms of imagery -- to suppress the image (a story begun by Akhnaton). Changing the position changes the meaning but also makes the image harder to grasp. The door of D -- almost like the entrance to a cave -- has been toppled sideways -- so we won't recognize it. Cave of the Nymphs -- Seven Sleepers -- king under the hill -- Sibyl -- dragon -- etc. Stay away from the chthonic: shun these sub-Lovecraftian cave dwellers. Don't deal with gnomes. D is for dead.

E

heh

hieroglyph

proto-sinaitic

phoenician

transition

E

is raising its hands to pray. Maybe E is for ecstasy: a whirling dervish in a Spiritismo church in New Orleans in 1923.

In cryptanalysis of coded documents presumed to be written in Indo-European of some sort the most frequently recurring sign is probably to be read as E. Fallen from its exalted state E prostrates itself, as the Professor says, towards horizontal earth, perhaps honoring the divine in everything -- transcendence to immanence. Here Comes Everybody.

Spectral E evokes the opposite of ecstasy: negative embodyment, sensation of body as tomb. Grade-B shriek of horror.

F

vav

hieroglyph

proto-Sinaitic

transition

F

for fetter. Actually nail, link, hammer. Also a burden (like a hobo's bindle). *De vinculis in genere*, the lid nailed shut, the sarcophagus of light.

Psyche pinned to velvet mounted inside a cube of glass in alphabetic order: vertebrae of the Encyclopaedia. At my back I hear Time's winged chariot, Artaud & Bruno at the stake signaling thru the flames. Angel of History, déja vu all over again.

Defixiones incised on lead & buried with the unquiet dead: double meaning of the word "spell." Tombstone of living speech, needle thru the wax genitalia: of course it only works if you believe in it. Against the evidence of our senses we're taught that night never falls. Jesus & the holy martyrs used it all up, the selfish bastards. You are not now nor have you ever slumped in trance nor salivated at the bells bells bells. All is clear. Your papers are in order. Dismissed.

Vav is a semitic link, "*and*", written in Arabic. But also but, so, as, etc. Such links make ideal nets, semantic traps, false identities, hallucinations.

23

G

zayin

hieroglyph

proto-sinaitic

phoenician

transition

G

weapon, face-to-face confrontation. The hieroglyph shows "flesh pierced by arrow."

Originally Z was the seventh letter but the Romans didn't need it & replaced it with G, a variant on the same Egypto-Semitic original; then later when they needed Z again they added it back at the end. Actually X should occupy the terminal position, since Y also came late around 50 BC.

What the world needs is more confrontation, Yeats shouted & banged the table at Coole Hall, alarming the dinner guests. Of course he was speaking as an occultist & not crypto-Blue shirt, or so we'd like to believe.

Against the infinite gravity of G we remember that violence once belonged to everybody but was finally monopolized by the State. Perhaps the State begins as a scapegoat carrying off our collective burden of bloodguilt into the sterile waste; -- hence war as the health of the State as Randolph Bourne put it, that hunchbacked anarchist.

Interlude: 1895. The naturalist John Burroughs gets up early &

25

walks out naked onto the adirondak/taoist porch of his cabin
Slabsides in the Esopus Hills puffing on a Marley-sized cone of
dagga & admiring the feng shui. A strange vortex of time & light
spirals down out of blue September & enfolds him; he vanishes.

When the State monopolized war it got control of peace as well.
What a surprise. No use blaming the dead, banging on the table &
blaming the dead. In Colombia some of the paramilitaries have
started arresting beating even killing people just for wearing
backward baseball hats. And how about those bass loudspeakers
mounted in cars so loud they threaten the very molecular sub-
structure of buildings, fibrillations of internal organs, birds
fall dead from trees, etc.? Dialectic? We don't need no
steenking dialectic.

Proudhon, after grokking the gist of Hegel in a few allnite
coffeebuzzed sessions with Young Marx (the Marx of the Philosophical
Notebooks) Paris 1844, decided to reject the dialectic altogether
in favor of a kind of unending existentialist confrontation or
contradiction No one has commented on the fact that Proudhon once
(in Bezançon) typeset a book on the Gnostic Dualists. The dialectic
itself is a trinitarian notion (Joachim di Fiore) as in the
sulphur mercury & salt of Paracelsus. Marx's family is said to've
had Frankist connections (Jakob Frank the Polish False Messiah who
apostasized to Catholicism the way Sabbatai Svi converted to Islam).
Maybe all ideas are Gnostic ideas, or is that idea too sarcastic?

Young handsome romantic Marx the Moor of the Carbonari.
Coins appeared around the same time as the perfect alphabet, the
Greek, the first to add written vowels. Consonants are not so much
sounds as ways of stopping sound. Only vowels really sound. Only
with the Greek alphabet is sound itself captured so that each
written word equals one spoken word, no more ambiguity. The coin
also represents one discrete unit of value or meaning. The alphabet
appears on the coin. The first image on a coin was the ox or bull.
Engraved with word & image the coin becomes an emblem (an
ideologized image), something like the personal lyric poem *written*
now for the first time rather than rhapsodized aloud, written on
paper to be seen, never to change. And yet change creeps in. The
coin is devalued, clipped, discounted, melted down for bullion.
Paleographic decay.

Consonantal alphabets like the Egypto-Sinaitic produce highly
personal texts in which memory must still play some role. "NL" could
mean nail, Nile, nil, Northern League, etc. etc. Scribal mysteries.
Greek letters are depersonalized & amnesiac -- democratized if you
prefer. Similarly commodity currency seems ambiguous & personal:
you could spend it or eat it (cattle, barley). But the coin
circulates without attachment, a floating signifier, permanent,
inedible, magically capable of reproducing or devaluing itself,
becoming debt, possessing but not possessed, hoarded, spent, gold
 & dung in a single rebus.

H

het

hieroglyph

proto-Canaanite

Transition

H

barrier, enclosure, fence, wall, confinement; sin (by a pun in
Hebrew, *het*). Once again they've tricked you by shifting the position
of the image so now it looks more like a simple wooden gate you
could slip under or hop over. The original hieroglyph looks much
more like prison bars.

H is a bad letter it seems. Once the Germans tried to get rid of
it. J. F. Hamann the magus of the North wrote a pamphlet in which
H defends itself in its own voice. Kabbalistic breath. In England
one slip of an H can ruin all chance of social progress. In English
our silent H's are rooted in phony French Norman snobbery. Our hours
spent in sad confinement.

Horus Apollo

It's a question of calling down daemons to inhabit statues so that
idolatry can be practised in the literal sense. Same in Tantra shastra.
The form captures or confines the spirit which thereupon becomes ours
to manipulate and/or worship. *Garland of Letters*. The alphabet failed
to exorcize these powers in fact as the Gematrist knows it made them
even fiercer. Bottle of djinn. But it also made them invisible or
rather so abstract that the literate mind soon forgot all original

29

imaginal links -- the hidden hieroglyphs. Each letter the prison or
birdcage of an angel. Matter exiled into bodilessness. Writing
began in secret because of its overtly blasphemous nature or rather
unnaturalness. You can be sure the devotees of Tiamat were
outraged. Writing was one of the 51 Principles of Civilization
that Inanna stole from the temple of Ea in Eridu & took back to
Uruch the city of Gilgamesh.

I Y J

yod

hieroglyph

proto-sinaitic

transition

IYJ

all share the same original hieroglyph showing an outstretched
hand or rather an arm with the palm turned up, a gesture like
begging, holding, giving, taking. Y was added in 50 BC and J not
until the 16th century in both cases to replace use of I as
consonant. Another hieroglyphic source for I -- "stylized bundle
of papyrus reeds" as used to make houses or boats -- and perhaps by
extension a roll of papyrus paper, a book or rather scroll. "To
demonstrate, command, show, count time, multiply, bless" -- so says
our Rabbi at the Aleph Center in Paris.

This is not healthy work. This is melancholy work -- under the
sign of Saturn. I need one of Ficino's remedies for this condition
something with musk crushed gold & jewels & perhaps blood or
hellebore. I. Je. Yo. Lie down naked on a bed of moss at Slabsides.

The I principle Ego & Its own: also captured & possessed by
alphabet, stained with it like the edge of a garment grasped by
a wheedling greasy beggar. Rolled up in a scroll, reified deified &
mystificatized. "I'm in control here" famous words of speedfreak
politician. Nemo put out my "I" says Cyclops.

32

Give me something against the waning of the Moon. A chimneysweep
for the spinal smoke hole of Kali the Snake.

K

kaf

hieroglyph

proto-Sinaitic

Transition

K

Palm of the Hand. Two fingers poked in the eyes of three stooges. Take give bless, the Three Graces or anti-stooges. Spectre & Form.

K the letter of Earth, X for Air, Z for Fire, Q for Water. Unspell these letters if you can. Disney characters have three fingers perhaps a hint of their demonic origin.

Lines on the palm of the hand as a possible source of letters: reading the palm, crossing it with silver. Dreams are the thing but not the thing: images words memories but not the thing. A doubling has occurred -- a doppelgänger in the invisible world of words -- and eventually this displacement goes so far that writing must be invented to contain restrain fixate & even kill the dream images like so many maggots. Contraction of awareness as defense against too much sensation. Gods no longer speak to us, the selfish bastards.

Palm of the hand -- Mother Hathor & her Five Daughters. Amun Ra in the empty original watery abyss of nothing-much-in-particular wanks off & cranks the universe -- "makes love to his hand" as the old texts put it. So the cosmos of scribes begins with jizm in the palm. The pen/is in the hand. Poem as lonely as a cloud.

Palm of the hand facing out & down: blessing: from the occult p.o.v. an actual etheric fluid flows from this gesture. Mesmerists made "passes" near the head or body of the patient. Anyone can do this but not everyone knows how to give without exhaustion of magnetism.

L

lamed

hieroglyph   (?)

proto-sinaitic   ∽

transition

ℓ ⋀ L

L

ox-goad; swiveling axis of the alphabet Libra the balance, the
Jeweled ankh of the cobra's treasure cave, the prick that sets all
in motion. King's sceptre fool's baton wizard's wand for dowsing.

Signifies study & teaching -- presumably because you have to be
goaded into it & locked up behind the schoolhouse door.

What does it mean to say that the Prophet was *unlettered*? literally
illiterate? So that Gabriel using yet another variant of the old
Egypto-Sinaitic abecedarium had to fill him up with letters like an
empty sack? there in the cave of the daemon of dreams? Or -- as certain
sufis allege -- because he'd gotten rid of the letters in some way,
transcended or absorbed them, erased them or washed them out in a
bowl of light? The Hurufiyya the original Lettrists created calligrammes
of Mohammed & Ali in which their faces & bodies are made of letters.
I have a behind-glass painting from Cirebon in Java in which the
body of the shadow-puppet clown Semar (albino hunchback hermaphrodite
dwarf) is composed of the Arabic letters ALLAH -- green & gold.

It helps to see the letters as both relative & absolute, so that

37

meaning changes with position & relation, as Bruno says -- but also
in a kabbalist sense "god-given." The fact now here uncovered: -- the
origin of the letters in occult Egyptian hieroglyphs -- reinforces
both points of view with divine ambiguity. To write against writing
means that one must write or else be written. The way down is the
way up the ladder of letters, like a pyramid of skulls.

M

mem

hieroglyph

proto-sinaitic

transition

M

water, moisture. The Egyptian hieroglyph of three horizontal zigzag line acts phonetically as MOO. Based on the noise a baby makes nursing many languages use the M sound for mother & milk. Hence lettristic or visual pun turns water-waves into breasts which are then rotated 180° from their iconic position

ᴄᴏ ᴍ in order once

again to disguise the letter's origin in a magic sign.

The zigzag-wave sign appears around 3500 BC in Ireland at the Brugh na Boinne (Newgrange etc.). All the Megalithic incised rocks are "abstract" hence indecipherable, giving them an uncanny impression of runic significance. Possibly these rocks act like Iroquois wampum: a kind of "pre"-writing of mnemonic devices that must be recalled & interpreted by experts like the Onondaga sachem who guarded the archive of major wampum "documents". The Effigy Mounds of Wisconsin (ca. 500 BC -1500 AD) can be recognized as animals or other shapes but remain otherwise untranslatable (unless some Winnebago elder secretly retains the keys) -- a kind of Koran of Nature written across an entire landscape. "Writing" may have appeared in this form many times without "evolving" into actual

writing in pictograms & ideograms. Why evolve? Writing brings with
it the miseries of the State, separation & alienation. The fact that
writing enables communication (hence action) at a distance -- like
magic -- not only destroys the Stone Age Sodality but was probably
intended to do so. Various forms of "pre"-writing (such as those
associated by M. Gimbutas with the Neolithic Goddess) should be
given a name that doesn't imply evolution-as-progress. Pre-literary
exists only from the perspective of literacy. "Memory glyphs" perhaps,
or "semi-semiotic sijils"? In any case such systems or non-systems
cannot be linked historically or archaeologically or anthropologically
to any of the cannibal cults that founded States (either in Old or
New World).

These mnemno glyphs, like wampum, usually belong to complex & wealthy
societies that developed ways of preventing the emergence of the
State or money or any other such witchcraft or blasphemy against the
great spirits. In other words these systems can be associated with the
Old Rights & Customs of the long Stone Age: roughly egalitarian
& waging only "primitive warfare" as Clastres called it, rather than
the classical warfare of the State, which aims at enslaving the
defeated. Iroquois war-captives were either killed or adopted into
the tribe. The Haudenosaunee League of Peace owned neither slaves
nor land; and wampum was neither "writing" nor "money".

Wm Burroughs once demanded of the State that it return all the colors it stole to animate its symbolic *imaginaire*: give back the green from the dollar bill to trees & grass, etc. The alphabet has also "stolen" symbols in order to perpetuate itself as the framework of a certain social relation. M has stolen the moisture out of baby's mouth. It should give back its waves to the sea & its breasts to the Goddess.

N

nun

hieroglyph

proto-Siniatic

Transition

N

fish or cobra. Our rabbi prefers fish because (he says) it follows logically after M for water -- and I suspect also because it's glatt kosher compared to the snake of snakes, poisonous, antediluvian, genital-like, glistening like a mine of jewels. Snakes are so non-monotheistic, rods of Egyptian magicians, friends of the druids, Nagas.

The "snake-worshippers" always live somewhere else, either in the next valley or in the distant time of ignorance. And everyone knows (without knowing) that "ignorance" here is priest-speak for "freedom", for the kind of sexual license & saturnalian excess that threatens all the rationalizations of the State. ("Marduk created you as His slaves," etc.). The killing of a Serpent always accompanies the triumphal bursting-forth of hierarchy & oppression. (The Chinese however merely tame their dragons & harness their energy. But then the Chinese never "evolved" an alphabet either.)

Anyway this fish, being hidden in the depths, stands for the occult here, same as the snake. The oldest known temple ever dug up by archaeologists -- the temple of Ea in Eridu (ca. 5000 BC) -- revealed that fish served as the usual sacrifice. Fish can be used against the Evil Eye, as can snakes.

N involves us in a certain necromantic miasma. Something has been killed by hiding it in the depths so deep we've lost its meaning. With the uraeus of N we're about to call up its spirit from the watery abyss or chaos that comprises the lost memory of the alphabet as a system of defixions. The crucified snake of the Ophites & Rosicrucians. The cobra like a living crown in Shiva's tangled locks

ayin

hieroglyph

proto-Sinaitic

Transition

O

the eye; spring, source of water. This identification exists in
other language families besides the Egypto-Semitic. Persian *cheshmeh*.
Eyes weep. Springs serve as eyes of the underworld -- hence
association of springs with nymphs or undines or djinn & later
with saints. This must be the Eye of Horus -- but right eye (solar)
or left eye (lunar)? I'd guess the latter which is linked with Thoth
the ibis-headed god of writing. In any case once more -- hidden
depths. The heroes of the Fenian Cycle often enter the world of faery
by plunging into springs. And the eye according to ancient optical
theory not only receives but sends rays. The shaman or magus can
transmit images to the (un)consciousness of others by direct gaze
like the hypnotist Svengali. In witchcraft this gaze becomes the Evil Eye
because we have TV and computer screen beaming out spells of greed envy
violence & replacing the human faculty of imagination with the crystalline
virus of money. Eye in the Pyramid the blind panopticon of Kapital.
Horus stumbling around like some grand guignol Boris Karloff mummy
in a fez moaning "O give me back my Eye!"

P

peh

hieroglyph

Semitic forms

Transition

P

the mouth. Easy to confuse the original hieroglyph with EYE and KNOT.

The Kabbalistic sense of the image here (& probably the Egyptian occult meaning) is "to read aloud" hence a book to be read, hence hermeneutics or active reading, *ta'wil*, taking a word or idea back to its source in order to unpack all its significance.

It's true we have here the picture of a smile. But a smile can cut both ways. Every letter a two-edged sword. For one thing the smile's been turned up on its edge; for another, it's attached to nothing -- like a Cheshire Cat.

Knot-magic is attested for archaic Semitic cultures & mentioned in early Arabic odes. Also very big in Shintoism in Japan. String figures (catscradles) (as collected by the late American surrealist Harry Smith) -- another possible source of letter-shapes & images. Bruno's *De vinculis* can also be read as knots. Binding is another technique for defixion, like letters scratched on lead or pins stuck in wax doll etc. Magical obstacles like the Gordian Knot. The mouth is stopped by invisible knots so the wizard's enemy is struck dumb.

Ultimately the alphabet impedes the kind of attentive or deep reading implied in the notion of reading aloud. Alphabetic literacy becomes a gestalt literacy, such that the letters no longer exist as separate entities, thus burying the images deeper & deeper in the unconscious.

Hittite cuneiform was first recognized as inscribing an Indo-European language when someone thought to read the pictogram for foot as the letter P or F since most I-E words for that limb (foot, paw, etc.) begin with one or the other of these nearly interchangeable sounds. I once suspected that both our P and F were pictograms for the foot (turned upside down naturally). But I'm now convinced that our rabbi's derivation of P from Egyptian to Proto-Sinaitic to "Chaldaean" (Phoenician) makes much better sense than my fanciful Hittite notion. Still perhaps a visual pun (maybe even a bi-lingual pun) was involved. The mouth -- let's face it -- is a nobler & "higher" organ than the foot, altho a mouth could kiss a foot -- either as slave or in voluntary amorous servitude as Fourier puts it so nicely.

The image of nourishment receives a positive inversion -- "not what goes in but what comes forth" -- inspired speech as food of the heart.

The negative inversion then would be speech as vomit: i.e., most speech. The same occult principle here as with palm-of-the-hand or *blessing*: imaginal emanations. Mantra shastra as sonic body of deity -- daemons -- embedded ideas -- phantasmata. Viva voce.

Note: Yantras, magical diagrams including the mandal (magic circle) Solomon's Seal, etc., should be considered possible sources of letters. Haitian *vévé*: each orisha has a "letter" that evokes because it "is" the presential form or active symbol of the voudoun. Something like this must've constituted the original "magical" origin legend of the hieroglyphs. On this point (as so many others) the magi like Athanasius Kircher or the author of the *Hypnerotomachia Poliphili* were right and Champollion was , well, not wrong, but unconscious. Science triumphs where steganography fails actually to decipher the hieroglyphs -- but by stressing the utilitarianism of the hieroglyph as used to indicate sound rather than meaning (Champollion's key in other words was thus "meaningless-ness"), science as usual slams the lid on any spooky mumia that might linger in the atmosphere from Late Antiquity -- those dreadfully superstitious neoplatonists like Porphyry & Iamblicus. Magical alphabet!? O dear no, merely a recycling of outworn pictograms as phonetic markers. Very scientific, given the primitive state of human reason, tho not much better than babies really.

Q

qof

hieroglyph

(heart &
Trachea)

proto-sinaitic

transition

Q

the ape. The hieroglyph shows a head & neck face forward but the
Hebrew name *qof* with ape, and maybe it's a monkey's face. Many
other hieroglyphs seem to've contributed to Q including heart-&-trachea,
eye-of-the-needle and cleaver. Hence the image of cutting or sewing,
separating & attaching. According to Horapollo the dog-faced ape
cynocephalus a kind of purple-assed baboon endemic to Egyptian temples
(like monkeys in India nowadays) was believed to keep time (i.e.,
to slice up the continuum of experience into measurable units) by
micturating on the very hour like a simian waterclock. Keeping time
not only resembles writing but requires it, hence the baboon embodies
Thoth or Hermes Trismegistus the inventor of writing. The cynocephalus
is a scribe. Writing is monkey business -- a million typewriters.

R

resh

hieroglyph

proto-sinaitic

transition

R

is for head, still quite recognizable simply facing the other way
& rather featureless like an egg-faced ghost in a Japanese horror
story.

The head signifies the beginning, like Ganesha, whose trunk we
might see in the righthand downward curve of the R. But the head
was never considered the sole seat of consciousness in archaic systems.
Heart & liver were also important (hence use of liver in Sumerian
divination) but in fact consciousness suffused the body & could
even be extended out of it by speech & other less obvious means.

Curiously, as Rev. Dodgson might've said, "modern science" may have
defenestrated the head as king of the galvanized cartesian corpse.
VR (virtual reality) simulations are predicated on a human reaction
time based on a certain lag between stimulus, and brain event, and
response. But it turns out that human reaction time seems much
quicker than that, maybe three times quicker. As if consciousness
were diffused thru the whole body, etc. The result: VR experiences
can cause motion sickness & even epilepsy. You might've been
wondering whatever became of virtual reality. The answer is: massive
lawsuits. Not even the military uses it much anymore apparently. The
Gulf War may turn out to've been its last application (& who knows,
maybe a cause of the "Gulf War Syndrome").

S

shin

hieroglyph

proto-Sinaitic

Transition

S

the teeth according to Kabbala but also related to the Egyptian
pictogram of mountains on the distant horizon meaning "bad."
In Sumerian the mountain glyph also had negative connotations
as "foreign" or "barbaric" since bad tribes lived up in them hills.
Like threatening teeth on a stranger's face.

Also bow-&-arrow, reminding us of Heraclitus's pun on *bios* as
bow, hence the tension of the pulled string or monochord, and *bios*
as life. The twanging of the magic twanger.

Probably each letter relates on principle to more than one
hieroglyph. Polysemantic ambiguity would be considered a source of
power. It would also suggest the formal/spectral dialectic, i.e.,
that each letter could have (as Amiri Baraka defines the dialectic)
a good side & a bad side. The archaeographic or hermeneutic task
would be to distinguish them and activate the positive. But how to
accomplish this without negation? etc. Historically the letters
have served to repress more than to express the powers they encapsulate
behind their hermetic seals. Like brushing cobwebs from a doorway.
(And shouldn't spiderwebs & the related art of weaving also be
considered possible sources for shapes of letters?)

57

T

tav

hieroglyph   ⚥   X

proto-Sinaitic   †   X

transition   †   T

T

the SIGN, from a hieroglyph for crossed sticks, probably one of
the very oldest (because obvious) semiotic devices. X marks the spot
-- who could doubt it? Neanderthals could've thought of this one.

Variations on the crucifixion. Both the X and the T were used as
well as the ✝ by those marvelously progressive Romans. And as
I'm sure you'd agree, Romans 'R' Us. We're still living in the
Roman Empire. The Vatican is the lineal descendent of the Roman
Empire as was the Holy version, the Russian version ("Third Rome")
the Ottoman version ("Rum" as in the poet Rumi) and England founded
by Brute the Trojan. Also Freemasonic America. We have Rome's laws,
especially its laws of property, essentially unchanged. We have its
alphabet. French Revolution as "Roman" republicanism. Eighteenth
century Classicism, i.e., the "Roman" view of Greece, as in "We are
all Greeks" -- something that could only've been said by a Roman --
or a German. Sure, the Empire declined, run down by vampiric taxation
& drainage of gold to the East more than barbaric invasions. Hey,
the barbarians *were* a kind of solution -- they embraced Romanismo
& injected élan vital into the decadent soup of empire. The barbarians
saved it. It never fell.

59

T and X as crossed sticks are signs of signness itself. Double-
distilled semiosis. Hence the imputation of extreme cruelty, the

"nailing down" aspect of letters carried to murderous terminality. Or from another p.o.v. the old Egyptian (African) custom of circumcision adopted as the sign of *the* covenant with G-d, that mysterious demon who tried to kill Moses but accepted his bloody foreskin thrown out of the tent. (Don't believe me? Read it in yer own Bible.)

As Semitic languages need several variants of T we have also *tet* and *tsadeh* from shield ⊗ and fishhook ∿ or anchor ↲ all of which seem related to our Graeco-Roman T. All could be interpreted according to hermetic-critical *ta'wil* as related to the science of letters. Words for example possess magical links like anchors with the things they represent (the multiplicity of languages doesn't disprove this notion because each language is language itself for its speakers), but letters hide or shield these essences, which must be fished up from the depths. Understanding has a cruel hooklike aspect, predatory & aggressive. Writing simultaneously reveals & withholds semantic meaning, whereas speech presents or expresses it -- not clearly (language is always unclear) but more-or-less directly at least. Everyone speaks but not everyone reads & writes: a distinction that 6000 years of "education" have not yet erased. As soon as writing appears the whole of oral/aural culture becomes "pre"-literate (& in fact is actively repressed -- altho archaeographology can dig up shards of it & reassemble them to some extent).

UVW

At the end of the alphabet a number of doublets & variants are
tacked on. U, V, and W are all versions of F the link
or *vav*, more chains in the grand spelling bee, the hex or jinx
system of literacy for the elite & TV for the masses. (How about a
deep reading or dense description of *TV Guide*?)

Y and Z

are spun off from K and G due to a bit of late tinkering with the system by non-initiates. Even so Z has become our Omega, hence the manifestation of the divine in matter: in that sense the summation of the doctrine of the alphabet as a possible praxis of liberation. Not just repression.

But in fact the actual last letter is (secretly) :

X

samekh

hieroglyph

transition

X

the ladder or support, based on a hieroglyph depicting a bundle
of reeds or bunch of stalks or possibly the skeleton of a fish,
or the backbone in general -- kundalini. The ladder of swords that
only the inspired shaman can climb in bare feet. The way up & out --
not (in our reading) out of matter but out of abstraction &
alienation & into reality -- that is, spirit & matter as one.
X the unknown. The alphabet as control imprisonment or weapon
against the self seems to be escapable only via the alphabet. Thus
far in agreement with Isou & Khlebnikov -- and of course with
Cabbala. Rimbaud's vowels, etc. A matter of stealing back the
hieroglyphs from those who stand to benefit (as de Nerval says)
from our ignorance of them.

X as Jack's beanstalk, the ladder to the Giant's treasure, held
hidden hostage above the clouds. The rescue of the treasure equals
the freeing of the Waters in the Rig Veda -- hence Soma the
efficacious sacrament of Indra & the inspired bard. Which raineth
as the gentle rain from heaven. But only because of the heroism
of the rescuer, in other words *himmah* or spiritual will, effort,
intentionality. A bathysphere for the A-B-Sea, hermeneutic balloon
ascent to seventh heaven.

Also (as "support"):

X

a picnic table.

Om Saraswati

Om Tara

the necklace of skulls